JAVASCRIPT

I0002458

THE SECRETS OF ASYNCHRONOUS PROGRAMMING ES6 AND BEYOND

OLIVER LUCAS JR

TABLE OF CONTENTS

Chapter 1

1.1 The Problem with Blocking Code
1.2 The Event Loop: JavaScript's Concurrency Manager
1.3 The Call Stack: JavaScript's Execution Tracker

Chapter 2

2.1 Callbacks: The Foundation of Asynchronous JavaScript
2.2 Nested Callbacks: When Asynchronous Operations Get Complex
2.3 Error-First Callbacks: The Convention

Chapter 3

3.1 Promises: A Better Way to Handle Asynchronicity
3.2 Promise Chaining: Creating Asynchronous Workflows
3.3 Handling Errors with Promises: .catch() and Beyond

Chapter 4

4.1 Async/Await: The Modern Approach to Asynchronous JavaScript
4.2 Error Handling with Try...Catch in Async/Await
4.3 Practical Use Cases for Async/Await

Chapter 5

5.1 Making HTTP Requests with Fetch API
5.2 JSON: The Language of Data Exchange
5.3 Handling AJAX Errors and Responses

Chapter 6

6.1 Iterators and Iterables: Unlocking Data One Step at a Time
6.2 Generators: Pausing and Resuming Execution
6.3 Real-World Applications of Generators

Chapter 7

7.1 Web Workers: JavaScript's Multithreading Solution
7.2 Communicating with Web Workers
7.3 Use Cases for Improved Performance

Chapter 8

8.1 Understanding the Observer Pattern
8.2 Building Custom Event Emitters
8.3 Practical Applications in Node.js

Chapter 9

9.1 Observables: Streams of Data Over Time
9.2 Observables as Asynchronous Streams
9.3 Building Reactive Applications

Chapter 10

10.1 Challenges in Testing Asynchronous Logic
10.2 Using Jest for Asynchronous Testing
10.3 Best Practices for Reliable Tests

Preface

In the ever-evolving landscape of web development, JavaScript stands as a cornerstone, empowering developers to create dynamic and interactive user experiences. And at the heart of modern JavaScript lies the fascinating world of asynchronous programming, a realm where actions unfold concurrently, shaping the responsiveness and efficiency of our applications.

This book, "JavaScript: The Secrets of Asynchronous Programming ES6 and Beyond," is your guide to mastering the intricacies of this essential paradigm. Whether you're a newcomer to JavaScript or a seasoned developer seeking to deepen your understanding, this book will equip you with the knowledge and skills to write clean, efficient, and maintainable asynchronous code.

We embark on this journey by unraveling the core concepts that underpin asynchronous JavaScript, exploring the event loop, the call stack, and the evolution of asynchronous patterns from callbacks to promises and async/await. We delve into the intricacies of AJAX, Web Workers, and event emitters, revealing their power in crafting responsive and high-performing applications.

As we progress, we venture into advanced territories, exploring asynchronous iteration, generators, and the reactive programming paradigm with RxJS. You'll learn to harness these powerful tools to manage complex asynchronous workflows and build truly reactive applications that respond seamlessly to data changes and user interactions.

Throughout this book, you'll find clear explanations, practical examples, and real-world use cases that illuminate the concepts and techniques discussed. We'll guide you through the challenges of testing asynchronous code and provide best practices for writing reliable and maintainable tests.

By the end of this journey, you'll not only have a deep understanding of asynchronous JavaScript but also the confidence to apply your knowledge to build the next generation of dynamic and interactive web experiences.

Welcome to the world of asynchronous JavaScript. Let's unlock its secrets together.

Chapter 1

Why Asynchronous?

1.1 The Problem with Blocking Code

The Single-Threaded Nature of JavaScript

JavaScript, at its core, is a single-threaded language. This means it can only execute one task at a time. Imagine a single worker in a factory who has to handle every step of a complex process sequentially. This worker can only do one thing at a time, and if one step takes a long time, everything else grinds to a halt.

Blocking the Flow

When JavaScript encounters a time-consuming operation, like fetching data from a server or reading a large file, it gets stuck. This is called "blocking" because the entire execution thread is blocked until that operation completes.

Think of it like this:

You're in line at the grocery store.

The person in front of you is paying with a check and it's taking forever.

Everyone behind them is stuck waiting, even if they just need to buy a single item.

This is what happens with blocking code in JavaScript. While the browser is waiting for a long-running task to finish, it can't respond to user interactions, update the page, or handle any other events. This leads to:

Unresponsive User Interfaces: The website appears frozen or sluggish, frustrating users.

Poor User Experience: Users might think the website is broken and leave.

Performance Bottlenecks: The entire application slows down, affecting efficiency.

Example: A Blocking Scenario

JavaScript

```javascript
console.log("Starting script...");

// Simulate a time-consuming task (e.g., fetching
data from a server)
function fetchData() {
  let result = 0;
    for (let i = 0; i < 1000000000; i++) { //
Simulate a long operation
      result += i;
  }
  return result;
}

const data = fetchData();
 console.log("Data fetched:", data);

console.log("Ending script...");
```

In this example, `fetchData()` simulates a long-running operation. While this function is executing, the browser is completely blocked. The messages "Starting script..." and "Ending script..." will only appear after `fetchData()` completes, which can take a noticeable amount of time.

The Need for Asynchronous Programming

To avoid these problems, JavaScript uses asynchronous programming. This allows the browser to handle multiple tasks concurrently without blocking the main thread. We'll explore the techniques for achieving this in the following chapters, starting with callbacks.

1.2 The Event Loop: JavaScript's Concurrency Manager

Imagine a tireless, efficient manager in a bustling office. This manager constantly monitors incoming tasks, prioritizes them, and ensures they're handled one by one without causing any bottlenecks. That's essentially the role of the event loop in JavaScript.

Even though JavaScript is single-threaded, the event loop allows it to handle asynchronous operations without blocking the main execution flow. It's the secret behind JavaScript's ability to stay responsive and manage multiple tasks seemingly at the same time.

How the Event Loop Works

1 Call Stack: When a JavaScript program starts, the event loop continuously monitors the call stack. The call stack is a LIFO (Last-In, First-Out) structure that keeps track of the currently executing functions. Each function call is added to the stack, and when a function completes, it's removed.

2 Web APIs/C++ APIs: When JavaScript encounters an asynchronous operation (like a timer, network request, or user input), it doesn't handle it directly. Instead, it delegates the task to Web APIs (provided by the browser environment) or C++ APIs (in Node.js). These APIs handle the operation in the background.

3 Callback Queue: Once an asynchronous operation is complete, the Web API or C++ API places a callback function (a function that's executed after the operation finishes) into the callback queue. This queue acts as a waiting area for tasks that are ready to be executed.

4 Event Loop's Role: The event loop continuously checks the call stack. If the call stack is empty (meaning no synchronous code is currently running), it takes the first callback function from the callback queue and pushes it onto the call stack for execution.

Visualizing the Event Loop

Think of it like this:

Call Stack: A restaurant kitchen where chefs prepare dishes one at a time.

Web APIs/C++ APIs: External suppliers delivering ingredients to the restaurant.

Callback Queue: A waiting area where the delivered ingredients are placed.

Event Loop: The head chef who checks if the kitchen is free and then grabs ingredients from the waiting area for the chefs to use.

Key Takeaways

The event loop is the heart of asynchronous JavaScript.

It allows JavaScript to handle multiple tasks concurrently without blocking the main thread.

The event loop continuously monitors the call stack and the callback queue to ensure smooth execution of code.

Understanding the event loop is crucial for writing efficient and responsive JavaScript applications.

In the next chapter, we'll look at callbacks, the traditional way of handling asynchronous operations in JavaScript.

1.3 The Call Stack: JavaScript's Execution Tracker

Imagine a stack of plates. When you add a plate, you place it on top. When you need a plate, you take the top one off. This is similar to how the call stack works in JavaScript. It's a fundamental concept that governs how functions are executed in your code.

LIFO (Last-In, First-Out)

The call stack operates on the LIFO principle (Last-In, First-Out). This means that the last function added to the stack is the first one to be executed and removed.

How the Call Stack Manages Function Execution

1 Global Execution Context: When your JavaScript code starts running, the environment creates a global execution context. This is the base environment where your code begins execution. It's like the foundation of your plate stack.

2 Function Calls: Every time you call a function, a new execution context is created for that function and pushed onto the top of the call stack. This context contains information about the function's local variables, arguments, and the code it needs to execute.

3 Execution: JavaScript executes the function that's currently on top of the call stack.

4 Returning Values: When a function completes its execution and returns a value (or implicitly returns `undefined`), its execution context is popped off the stack.

5 Stack Trace: If an error occurs during execution, the call stack provides a "stack trace." This trace shows the sequence of function calls that led to the error, making it easier to debug.

Example: Visualizing the Call Stack

JavaScript

```
function greet(name) {
    console.log("Hello, " + name + "!");
}

function introduce(name, age) {
    greet(name);
    console.log("I am " + age + " years old.");
}

introduce("Alice", 30);
```

Here's how the call stack would look during the execution of this code:

Global Execution Context: The script starts, and the global execution context is pushed onto the stack.

`introduce("Alice", 30)`: `introduce()` is called, and its context is pushed onto the stack.

`greet(name)`: Inside `introduce()`, `greet("Alice")` is called, and its context is pushed onto the stack.

`console.log("Hello, Alice!")`: `greet()` executes its code, printing "Hello, Alice!". `greet()`'s context is popped off the stack.

```
console.log("I am 30 years old."): introduce()
```
continues executing, printing "I am 30 years old.". `introduce()`'s context is popped off the stack.

Global Execution Context: The script finishes, and the global execution context is popped off the stack.

Key Takeaways

The call stack is a crucial mechanism for managing function execution in JavaScript.

It operates on the LIFO principle, ensuring that functions are executed in the correct order.

Understanding the call stack is essential for debugging and writing efficient code.

The call stack is a synchronous process. Each function must complete before the next one can begin. This is where the event loop and asynchronous programming come into play, which we'll explore further.

Chapter 2

Callbacks: The Old Way

2.1 Callbacks: The Foundation of Asynchronous JavaScript

Callbacks are the original way JavaScript handled asynchronous operations. They are functions that are passed as arguments to other functions and are executed after the first function completes. This allows you to perform actions after an asynchronous operation finishes without blocking the main thread.

How Callbacks Work

1 Passing a Function as an Argument: You define a function (the callback) that you want to execute later. This function is passed as an argument to another function that performs an asynchronous operation.

2 Asynchronous Operation: The main function initiates the asynchronous task, like fetching data from a server or setting a timer.

3 Execution Upon Completion: Once the asynchronous operation is complete, the main function "calls back" the callback function, providing any necessary data as arguments.

Example: setTimeout with a Callback

JavaScript

```
console.log("Before setTimeout");
```

```
setTimeout(function() {
  console.log("Inside the callback function");
}, 2000); // Execute the callback after 2 seconds

console.log("After setTimeout");
```

In this example:

`setTimeout` is an asynchronous function that waits for a specified time (2 seconds here).

The anonymous function `function() { console.log("Inside the callback function"); }` is the callback.

Output:

"Before setTimeout" is logged first.

"After setTimeout" is logged second.

After 2 seconds, "Inside the callback function" is logged.

This demonstrates that the code doesn't block while waiting for the timer.

Callbacks in Real-World Scenarios

Event Handling: Callbacks are used extensively for handling user interactions like clicks, mouseovers, and keyboard input.

AJAX Requests: Callbacks handle responses from web servers after data is fetched.

Node.js: Callbacks are fundamental to Node.js for handling I/O operations, like reading files or interacting with databases.

Limitations of Callbacks

While callbacks are essential, they have drawbacks:

Callback Hell: Nested callbacks can lead to deeply indented, difficult-to-read code (often called the "pyramid of doom").

Error Handling: Managing errors with callbacks can become complex, especially in nested structures.

These limitations led to the development of promises and async/await, which provide more structured and manageable ways to handle asynchronous operations. We'll explore those in the upcoming chapters.

2.2 Nested Callbacks: When Asynchronous Operations Get Complex

Callbacks are great for simple asynchronous tasks. But what happens when you need to perform multiple asynchronous operations in sequence? This is where nested callbacks come into play, and potentially, callback hell.

The Scenario

Imagine you need to:

1 Read a file from the file system.

2 Process the data from that file.

3 Make an API request with the processed data.

4 Update the user interface with the API response.

Each of these steps is asynchronous. Using callbacks, you'd need to nest them within each other, as each step depends on the previous one completing.

Example: Nested Callbacks

JavaScript

```javascript
fs.readFile('data.txt', 'utf8', (err, data) => {
  if (err) {
    console.error("Failed to read file:", err);
    return;
  }

  // Process the data
  const processedData = processData(data);

  // Make an API request
        makeApiRequest(processedData,        (err,
apiResponse) => {
    if (err) {
      console.error("API request failed:", err);
      return;
    }

    // Update the UI
    updateUI(apiResponse);
  });
});
```

The Problem: Callback Hell

As you add more asynchronous steps, the nesting gets deeper and deeper, leading to code that:

Is hard to read and understand: The indentation becomes excessive, making it difficult to follow the flow of execution.

Is difficult to debug: Tracking down errors becomes a nightmare, as you have to trace through multiple levels of nested functions.

Is difficult to maintain: Making changes or adding new features becomes complex and error-prone.

This deeply nested structure is often called the "pyramid of doom" or "callback hell."

Why Callback Hell is a Problem

Cognitive Overload: Our brains are not designed to easily process deeply nested structures. This makes it harder to understand the logic and increases the chance of errors.

Maintainability Nightmare: Imagine trying to add a step in the middle of a deeply nested callback chain. It becomes a tedious and error-prone task.

Error Handling Complexity: Properly handling errors in nested callbacks can be challenging, as you need to ensure that errors are caught and handled at the appropriate level.

Solutions

Fortunately, there are solutions to escape callback hell:

Promises: Promises provide a more structured way to handle asynchronous operations, allowing you to chain them and handle errors more effectively.

Async/Await: Async/await builds on promises and makes asynchronous code look and behave a bit more like synchronous code, further improving readability and maintainability.

We'll explore these solutions in the next chapters.

2.3 Error-First Callbacks: The Convention

In Node.js and many JavaScript libraries, a common pattern for handling errors in callbacks is the "error-first" callback. This convention makes error handling more explicit and predictable.

How it Works

1 Error Parameter: The first argument to the callback function is reserved for an error object. If an error occurs during the asynchronous operation, this object will contain information about the error. If no error occurred, it will be `null` or `undefined`.

2 Result Parameter: The subsequent arguments to the callback function are for the results of the successful operation.

Example: Error-First Callback

JavaScript

```javascript
function readFile(filename, callback) {
  // Simulate reading a file (could be an actual
file system operation)
  if (filename === 'nonexistent.txt') {
    const err = new Error('File not found');
    callback(err, null); // Pass the error object
as the first argument
  } else {
    const data = "File contents";
    callback(null, data); // Pass null for error
and the data as the result
  }
}

readFile('data.txt', (err, data) => {
  if (err) {
    console.error("Failed to read file:", err);
    return;
  }
  console.log("File data:", data);
});
```

Benefits of Error-First Callbacks

Consistency: Provides a standard way to handle errors across different libraries and modules.

Explicitness: Makes it clear that error handling is an important part of the callback function.

Early Exit: Allows you to handle errors immediately at the beginning of the callback, preventing further execution if needed.

Handling Errors in Nested Callbacks

Even with error-first callbacks, error handling in nested callbacks can be tricky. You need to make sure errors are propagated correctly through each level of nesting.

JavaScript

```javascript
function step1(callback) {
  // ... some asynchronous operation ...
  if (error) {
    callback(error);
  } else {
    callback(null, result1);
  }
}


function step2(result1, callback) {
  // ... another asynchronous operation ...
  if (error) {
    callback(error);
  } else {
    callback(null, result2);
  }
}
```

```
step1((err, result1) => {
  if (err) {
    console.error("Error in step 1:", err);
    return;
  }

  step2(result1, (err, result2) => {
    if (err) {
      console.error("Error in step 2:", err);
      return;
    }
    // ... continue with result2 ...
  });
});
```

Challenges with Error Handling in Callbacks

Error Propagation: Ensuring that errors are passed correctly through multiple levels of nested callbacks can be cumbersome.

Code Complexity: Error handling logic can make nested callbacks even more difficult to read and maintain.

This complexity is one of the main reasons why promises and async/await were introduced in JavaScript. They offer a more structured and manageable approach to error handling in asynchronous code.

Chapter 3

Promises: A Better Approach

3.1 Promises: A Better Way to Handle Asynchronicity

Promises provide a more elegant and manageable way to deal with asynchronous operations in JavaScript compared to traditional callbacks. They represent the eventual result of an asynchronous operation, whether it's a success or failure.

The Promise Object

A promise is an object that can be in one of three states:

Pending: The initial state of a promise. The asynchronous operation is still in progress.

Fulfilled (Resolved): The operation completed successfully, and the promise now holds a value (the result of the operation).

Rejected: The operation failed, and the promise now holds an error object (representing the reason for failure).

Creating a Promise

You create a promise using the `Promise` constructor:

JavaScript

```
const myPromise = new Promise((resolve, reject)
=> {
   // Perform an asynchronous operation (e.g.,
fetch data, timer)
   if (operationSuccessful) {
```

```
    resolve(result);  // Resolve with the result
value
  } else {
    reject(error);      // Reject with an error
object
  }
});
```

The constructor takes a function with two arguments:

`resolve`: A function to call when the operation is successful, passing the result value.

`reject`: A function to call when the operation fails, passing an error object.

Promise Methods

Promises provide methods for handling the outcome of an asynchronous operation:

`.then()`: Used to handle the successful fulfillment of a promise. It takes a callback function that receives the resolved value as an argument.

JavaScript

```
myPromise.then(result => {
  console.log("Promise resolved with:", result);
});
```

`.catch()`: Used to handle rejections (errors) of a promise. It takes a callback function that receives the error object as an argument.

JavaScript

```javascript
myPromise.catch(error => {
  console.error("Promise rejected with:", error);
});
```

`.finally()`: Takes a callback function that is always executed, regardless of whether the promise is fulfilled or rejected. Useful for cleanup tasks.

JavaScript

```javascript
myPromise.finally(() => {
    console.log("Promise settled (fulfilled or rejected)");
});
```

Benefits of Promises

Improved Readability: Promises reduce the nesting and complexity associated with callbacks, making code easier to read and understand.

Better Error Handling: The `.catch()` method provides a clear and centralized way to handle errors.

Chaining: Promises can be chained using `.then()`, allowing you to perform a series of asynchronous operations in a more structured manner.

In the next chapter, we'll explore how to chain promises for more complex asynchronous workflows.

3.2 Promise Chaining: Creating Asynchronous Workflows

One of the most powerful features of promises is the ability to chain them together. This allows you to execute a sequence of asynchronous operations in a more readable and organized way, avoiding the nesting issues of callbacks.

How Promise Chaining Works

1 Returning Promises: Each `.then()` method of a promise should return another promise. This creates a chain where each subsequent `.then()` handles the result of the previous promise.

2 Sequential Execution: The promises in the chain are executed in sequence, ensuring that one operation completes before the next one starts.

3 Passing Data Along: You can pass data from one promise to the next by returning values from the `.then()` callbacks.

Example: Chaining Promises

JavaScript

```
function fetchData() {
  return new Promise((resolve, reject) => {
    // Simulate fetching data from a server
    setTimeout(() => {
```

```javascript
      const data = { name: "Alice", age: 30 };
      resolve(data);
    }, 1000);
  });
}

function processData(data) {
  return new Promise((resolve, reject) => {
    // Simulate processing the data
    setTimeout(() => {
      const processedData = `Name: ${data.name},
Age: ${data.age}`;
      resolve(processedData);
    }, 500);
  });
}

function displayData(processedData) {
  console.log("Processed Data:", processedData);
}

// Chain the promises
fetchData()
  .then(data => {
      return processData(data); // Return a new
promise
  })
  .then(processedData => {
    displayData(processedData);
  })
  .catch(error => {
    console.error("Error:", error);
  });
```

In this example:

`fetchData()` simulates fetching data and returns a promise that resolves with the data.

`processData()` simulates processing the data and returns a promise that resolves with the processed data.

`displayData()` logs the processed data to the console.

The promises are chained using `.then()`, ensuring that data is fetched, then processed, then displayed.

Benefits of Promise Chaining

Improved Readability: Chaining makes asynchronous code flow more linearly and clearly, avoiding nested structures.

Easier Debugging: It's easier to track the flow of data and identify errors in a chained structure.

Better Error Handling: A single `.catch()` at the end of the chain can handle errors from any of the promises in the chain.

Chaining and Async/Await

Promise chaining provides a significant improvement over callbacks. However, async/await, which we'll cover next, takes this a step further by making asynchronous code look and behave even more like synchronous code.

3.3 Handling Errors with Promises: .catch() and Beyond

Promises offer a more structured and cleaner way to handle errors in asynchronous JavaScript compared to traditional callbacks. Here's how you can effectively manage errors using promises:

.catch() Method

The `.catch()` method is the primary way to handle rejections (errors) in promises. It acts as a dedicated error handler for the entire promise chain.

JavaScript

```
somePromise
  .then(result => {
    // ... process result ...
  })
  .catch(error => {
    console.error("An error occurred:", error);
    // ... handle the error (e.g., display an error message, retry) ...
  });
```

Error Propagation in Chains

If an error occurs in any of the `.then()` blocks in a promise chain, the control flow immediately jumps to the nearest `.catch()` block. This means you don't need to handle errors in every `.then()`, simplifying your code.

JavaScript

```
promise1()
  .then(result1 => {
    // ...
    return promise2(result1);
  })
  .then(result2 => {
    // ...
    return promise3(result2);
```

```
  })
  .catch(error => {
    // Handles errors from promise1, promise2, or
promise3
    console.error("Error in the chain:", error);
  });
```

Throwing Errors in Promises

You can throw errors within a `.then()` block to signal a rejection. This will also trigger the `.catch()` handler.

JavaScript

```
promise1()
  .then(result => {
    if (result.hasError) {
      throw new Error("Invalid data received");
    }
    // ... process result ...
  })
  .catch(error => {
    // ... handle the error ...
  });
```

Handling Errors in .then()

While `.catch()` is the preferred way, you can also handle errors directly within a `.then()` block by providing a second callback function:

JavaScript

```
promise1()
```

```
.then(
  result => { /* handle success */ },
  error => { /* handle error */ }
);
```

Important Considerations

Always Use .catch(): It's a best practice to always include a `.catch()` at the end of your promise chains to handle any unexpected errors.

Specific Error Handling: For more fine-grained control, you can use multiple `.catch()` blocks to handle different types of errors differently.

Async/Await and try...catch: When using async/await, you can use familiar `try...catch` blocks to handle errors in asynchronous code, which we'll cover in detail later.

By using promises and their error-handling mechanisms effectively, you can write more robust and maintainable asynchronous JavaScript code.

Chapter 4

Async/Await: Modern Asynchronicity

4.1 Async/Await: The Modern Approach to Asynchronous JavaScript

Async/await is a powerful feature in modern JavaScript that allows you to write asynchronous code that looks and behaves a bit more like synchronous code. It builds on top of promises, making them easier to use and reason about.

The `async` **Keyword**

Declaring Asynchronous Functions: You use the `async` keyword before a function declaration to indicate that the function is asynchronous. An `async` function always implicitly returns a promise.

JavaScript

```
async function myAsyncFunction() {
  // ... asynchronous code ...
}
```

The `await` **Keyword**

Pausing for Promises: Inside an `async` function, you can use the `await` keyword before a promise. This pauses the execution of the function until the promise is resolved, and then returns the resolved value.

JavaScript

```
async function myAsyncFunction() {
  const result = await somePromise;
  // ... code that uses the result ...
}
```

Example: Async/Await in Action

JavaScript

```
function fetchData() {
  return new Promise(resolve => {
    setTimeout(() => {
      const data = { name: "Alice", age: 30 };
      resolve(data);
    }, 1000);
  });
}

async function processData() {
  const data = await fetchData(); // Wait for
fetchData to resolve
  console.log("Data:", data);
  // ... process the data ...
}

processData();
```

Benefits of Async/Await

Cleaner Code: Async/await eliminates the need for `.then()` chains, making asynchronous code more concise and readable.

Synchronous-like Flow: The `await` keyword allows you to write asynchronous code that flows more like synchronous code, making it easier to follow.

Error Handling with try...catch: You can use standard `try...catch` blocks to handle errors in `async` functions, just like in synchronous code.

Error Handling with Async/Await

JavaScript

```javascript
async function processData() {
  try {
    const data = await fetchData();
    // ... process data ...
  } catch (error) {
    console.error("Error:", error);
  }
}
```

Important Notes

`async` **Functions Always Return Promises:** Even if you don't explicitly return a promise from an `async` function, it will implicitly return a promise that resolves with the function's return value.

`await` **Only Works Inside** `async` **Functions:** You can only use the `await` keyword within functions declared with `async`.

Async/await is a powerful tool for writing cleaner, more manageable asynchronous code in JavaScript. It simplifies the structure and makes asynchronous logic easier to reason about.

4.2 Error Handling with Try...Catch in Async/Await

Async/await makes error handling in asynchronous JavaScript code much more intuitive by allowing you to use the familiar try...catch blocks, just like you would in synchronous code.

How it Works

1 Wrap Asynchronous Code in try: Place the code that might throw an error inside a try block.

2 Handle Errors in catch: If an error occurs within the try block, the execution jumps to the catch block. The catch block receives an error object that provides information about the error.

Example: Async/Await with Try...Catch

JavaScript

```
async function fetchData() {
    // Simulate fetching data (could throw an
error)
    return new Promise((resolve, reject) => {
        if (Math.random() < 0.5) { // Simulate a 50%
chance of error
            reject(new Error("Network error"));
        } else {
        setTimeout(() => {
            resolve({ name: "Alice", age: 30 });
        }, 1000);
        }
    });
}

async function processData() {
```

```
  try {
    const data = await fetchData(); // Wait for
the promise
    console.log("Data:", data);
    // ... process the data ...
  } catch (error) {
    console.error("Error fetching data:", error);
     // ... handle the error (e.g., display an
error message, retry) ...
  }
}

processData();
```

Benefits of Using Try...Catch with Async/Await

Clear and Concise: Error handling logic is grouped within the `try...catch` block, making it easy to read and understand.

Synchronous-like Handling: You handle errors in the same way you would in synchronous code, making it more intuitive for developers.

Improved Code Structure: `try...catch` blocks help to separate error handling from the main logic of your asynchronous code.

Important Notes

`async` **Functions and Promises:** Remember that `async` functions always return promises. If an error is thrown inside an `async` function and not caught by a `try...catch` block, the promise returned by the function will be rejected with that error.

Error Propagation: If you don't use a `try...catch` block within an `async` function, any unhandled errors will propagate up to the caller of the function.

By combining async/await with `try...catch` blocks, you can write asynchronous JavaScript code that is not only cleaner and more readable but also more robust and reliable.

4.3 Practical Use Cases for Async/Await

Async/await shines in many real-world scenarios where you need to manage asynchronous operations effectively.[1] Here are some practical use cases:

1. Simplifying Asynchronous API Calls

Fetching data from APIs is a common task in web development.[2] Async/await makes it much cleaner:[3]

JavaScript

```javascript
async function getWeatherData(city) {
  try {
                const        response    =       await
fetch(`https://api.weatherapi.com/v1/current.json
?key=YOUR_API_KEY&q=${city}`);
    const data = await response.json();
    return data;
  } catch (error) {
    console.error("Error fetching weather data:",
error);
  }
}
```

2. User Interface Interactions

Async/await can improve the user experience by preventing the UI from freezing during long operations:

JavaScript

```
async function handleSubmit(event) {
  event.preventDefault(); // Prevent default form
submission
  showLoader(); // Display a loading indicator

  try {
            const    response    =    await
submitFormData(formData);
    // Update UI with success message or results
  } catch (error) {
    // Display error message to the user
  } finally {
    hideLoader(); // Hide the loading indicator
  }
}
```

3. Reading and Writing Files (Node.js)

In Node.js, file system operations are asynchronous.[4] Async/await simplifies working with files:

JavaScript

```
const fs = require('fs').promises; // Use the
promises version of fs

async function readFile(filename) {
  try {
```

```
      const  data  =  await  fs.readFile(filename,
'utf8');
    return data;
  } catch (error) {
    console.error("Error reading file:", error);
  }
}
```

4. Concurrent Operations with `Promise.all`

Async/await works seamlessly with `Promise.all` to execute multiple asynchronous operations concurrently:

JavaScript

```
async function fetchMultipleData() {
  try {
        const  [data1,  data2,  data3]  =  await
Promise.all([
      fetch('/api/data1'),
      fetch('/api/data2'),
      fetch('/api/data3')
    ]);
    // Process data1, data2, data3
  } catch (error) {
    // Handle any errors
  }
}
```

5. Timers and Timeouts

Async/await can make working with timers more readable:

JavaScript

```
async function delay(ms) {
        return       new       Prcmise(resolve       =>
setTimeout(resolve, ms));
}

async function doSomething() {
  await delay(2000); // Wait for 2 seconds
  // ... code to execute after the delay ...
}
```

Key Takeaways

Async/await makes asynchronous code more readable and easier to reason about.[5]

It helps to prevent blocking the main thread, improving the responsiveness of your applications.[6]

Async/await integrates well with other asynchronous patterns like `Promise.all`.

By using async/await effectively, you can write cleaner, more efficient, and more maintainable asynchronous JavaScript code.[7]

Chapter 5

Working with AJAX

5.1 Making HTTP Requests with Fetch API

The Fetch API is a modern interface in JavaScript that provides a powerful and flexible way to make HTTP requests to servers from web browsers. It's a significant improvement over the older `XMLHttpRequest` object, offering a more concise and promise-based approach.

Basic Fetch Request

The core of the Fetch API is the `fetch()` method. Here's a simple example of a GET request:

JavaScript

```javascript
fetch('https://api.example.com/data')

  .then(response => {

    // Handle the response

    console.log(response);

})

  .catch(error => {

    // Handle any errors
```

```
        console.error('Error:', error);

    });
```

Understanding the Response

The `fetch()` method returns a promise that resolves to a `Response` object. This object contains information about the response from the server, including:

`status`: The HTTP status code (e.g., 200 for OK, 404 for Not Found).

`statusText`: The status message corresponding to the status code.

`headers`: An object containing the response headers.

`ok`: A boolean indicating whether the response was successful (status code in the range 200-299).

Accessing the Response Body

The `Response` object provides methods to access the body of the response in various formats:

`text()`: Returns a promise that resolves with the response body as text.

`json()`: Returns a promise that resolves with the response body parsed as JSON.

`blob()`: Returns a promise that resolves with the response body as a Blob (binary data).

`formData()`: Returns a promise that resolves with the response body as FormData.

`arrayBuffer()`: Returns a promise that resolves with the response body as an ArrayBuffer (raw binary data).

Example: Fetching JSON data

JavaScript

```javascript
fetch('https://api.example.com/data')

  .then(response => response.json())

  .then(data => {

    console.log(data); // Access the parsed JSON data

  })

  .catch(error => {

    console.error('Error:', error);

  });
```

Making POST Requests

To make a POST request, you need to provide an `init` object as the second argument to `fetch()`. This object allows you to specify the HTTP method, headers, and body of the request.

JavaScript

```javascript
const data = { name: 'Alice', age: 30 };
```

```javascript
fetch('https://api.example.com/data', {

  method: 'POST',

  headers: {

    'Content-Type': 'application/json'

  },

  body: JSON.stringify(data)

})

  .then(response => response.json())

  .then(data[1] => {

    // Handle the response

  })

  .catch(error[2] => {

    // Handle errors

  });
```

Key Considerations

Error Handling: The `fetch()` promise only rejects for network errors. You need to check the `response.ok` property or the `status` code to handle HTTP errors (e.g., 400 Bad Request, 500 Internal Server Error).

CORS: Be mindful of Cross-Origin Resource Sharing (CORS) policies when making requests to different domains.

Async/Await: Combine `fetch()` with async/await for even cleaner asynchronous code:

JavaScript

```
async function fetchData() {

  try {

            const      response      =      await
fetch('https://api.example.com/data');

    const data = await response.json();[3]

    // ... use the data ...

  } catch (error) {

    // ... handle errors ...

  }

}
```

The Fetch API provides a modern and efficient way to make HTTP requests in JavaScript, simplifying interactions with web services and APIs.

5.2 JSON: The Language of Data Exchange

JSON (JavaScript Object Notation) has become the standard format for sending and receiving data between web clients and servers. Its lightweight, human-readable structure and compatibility with JavaScript make it ideal for API interactions.

Sending JSON Data

When you need to send data to a server, such as submitting form data, creating a new resource, or updating existing data, you often send it in JSON format. Here's how you do it with the Fetch API:

Create a JavaScript Object: Represent the data you want to send as a JavaScript object.

JavaScript

```
const newUserData = {

    name: "Alice",

    email: "alice@example.com",

    age: 30

};
```

Set the `Content-Type` **Header:** In the `fetch()` call, set the `Content-Type` header to `application/json` to indicate that you're sending JSON data.

Stringify the Object: Use `JSON.stringify()` to convert the JavaScript object into a JSON string.

Include the JSON String in the Request Body: Pass the JSON string as the `body` of the `fetch()` request.

Example: Sending JSON data with a POST request

JavaScript

```javascript
fetch('https://api.example.com/users', {

  method: 'POST',

  headers: {

    'Content-Type': 'application/json'

  },

  body: JSON.stringify(newUserData)

})

  .then(response => {

    // Handle the response

  })
```

```
.catch(error => {

  // Handle errors

});
```

Receiving JSON Data

When a server sends you data in JSON format, you need to parse it to use it in your JavaScript code.

Use `response.json()`: After making a `fetch()` request, use the `response.json()` method. This method returns a promise that resolves with the parsed JSON data as a JavaScript object.

Example: Receiving and using JSON data

JavaScript

```
fetch('https://api.example.com/users/123')

  .then(response => response.json())

  .then(userData => {

        console.log(userData.name);   // Access
properties of the parsed JSON object

    console.log(userData.email);

  })

  .catch(error => {
```

```
// Handle errors

});
```

Key Considerations

Data Validation: Always validate the received JSON data to ensure it has the expected structure and data types before using it in your application.

Error Handling: Handle potential errors during both sending and receiving JSON data, such as invalid JSON format or network issues.

Security: Be mindful of security best practices when sending and receiving data, especially sensitive information.

By understanding how to send and receive JSON data effectively, you can build robust and dynamic web applications that interact seamlessly with APIs and backend services.

5.3 Handling AJAX Errors and Responses

Handling AJAX errors and responses effectively is crucial for building robust and user-friendly web applications. Here's a breakdown of how to handle different scenarios using the Fetch API:

1. Network Errors

Network errors occur when there's a problem with the connection, such as the server being unavailable or the user being offline. The `fetch()` method will reject its promise in these cases.

JavaScript

```javascript
fetch('https://api.example.com/data')

  .then(response => {

    // ... handle the response ...

  })

  .catch(error => {

    console.error('Network error:', error);

    // Display an error message to the user,

        // suggest checking their internet
connection, etc.

  });
```

2. HTTP Errors

Even if the request reaches the server, it might not be successful. The server can respond with various HTTP error status codes (e.g., 400 Bad Request, 404 Not Found, 500 Internal Server Error).

JavaScript

```javascript
fetch('https://api.example.com/data')

  .then(response => {

    if (!response.ok) {
```

```javascript
    // HTTP error occurred

    if (response.status === 404) {

        console.error('Resource not found');

            // Display a specific message for a 404
error

    } else {

                console.error('HTTP  error:',
response.status, response.statusText);

        // Handle other HTTP errors

    }

        // Optionally, throw an error to trigger
the .catch() block

            throw  new  Error('HTTP  error  '  +
response.status);

    }

    return response.json(); // Parse the response
if successful

    })

    .then(data => {

    // ... process the data ...
```

```
})

.catch(error => {

    console.error('Error:', error); // Catch
network errors or thrown HTTP errors

    // Display a generic error message to the
user

});
```

3. Handling Different Response Types

APIs can return different types of data (JSON, text, Blob, etc.). You need to handle them accordingly:

JavaScript

```
fetch('https://api.example.com/data')

  .then(response => {

    if (!response.ok) {

      // ... handle HTTP errors ...

    }

            const contentType =
response.headers.get('content-type');
```

```javascript
                    if       (contentType      &&
contentType.includes('application/json')) {

      return response.json();[1]

            }    else    if    (contentType      &&
contentType.includes('text/plain')) {

      return response.text();[2]

  } else {

    // Handle other content types or unexpected
responses

        console.error('Unexpected content type:',
contentType);

    }

  })

  .then(data => {

    // ... process the data based on its type ...

  })

  .catch(error => {

    // ... handle errors ...

  });
```

4. Displaying User-Friendly Messages

Provide informative and user-friendly error messages to guide the user:

Specific Error Messages: When possible, display specific error messages based on the type of error (e.g., "Invalid username or password," "Resource not found").

Generic Error Messages: For unexpected errors, provide a generic message like "An error occurred. Please try again later."

Avoid Exposing Sensitive Information: Don't display detailed error messages that might reveal sensitive information about your server or application.

5. Using Async/Await

Combine the Fetch API with async/await for cleaner error handling:

JavaScript

```
async function fetchData() {

  try {

            const response = await
fetch('https://api.example.com/data');

    if (!response.ok) {

      // ... handle HTTP errors ...

    }
```

```
    const data = await response.json();

    // ... process the data ...

  } catch (error) {

    console.error('Error:', error);

    // ... display an error message to the user
...

  }

}
```

By following these guidelines, you can create more robust and user-friendly web applications that handle AJAX errors gracefully and provide a better user experience.

Chapter 6

Asynchronous Iteration and Generators

6.1 Iterators and Iterables: Unlocking Data One Step at a Time

Iterators and iterables are fundamental concepts in JavaScript that provide a standardized way to traverse or loop over sequences of data, such as arrays, strings, maps, and sets.[1] They are especially useful in asynchronous programming when dealing with streams of data or when you need to process data in chunks.

Iterables

Definition: An iterable is any object that implements the iterable protocol. This means the object has a special method called `Symbol.iterator` that returns an iterator.

Purpose: Iterables provide a way to access the data they hold sequentially, without exposing the underlying implementation details.

Examples: Arrays, strings, maps, sets, and even custom objects can be iterables.

Iterators

Definition: An iterator is an object that implements the iterator protocol.[2] This means it has a `next()` method that returns an object with two properties:

`value`: The next value in the sequence.

`done:` A boolean indicating whether there are more values to iterate over.

Purpose: Iterators keep track of the current position in the sequence and provide a way to fetch the next value.[3]

The Iteration Process

1 Obtain an Iterator: Call the `Symbol.iterator` method on the iterable object to get an iterator.

2 Call `next()`: Repeatedly call the `next()` method on the iterator to retrieve each value in the sequence.

3 Check `done:` The `done` property of the returned object tells you when you've reached the end of the sequence.

Example: Iterating over an Array

JavaScript

```
const myArray = [1, 2, 3];

const iterator = myArray[Symbol.iterator]();
```

```
console.log(iterator.next());  // { value: 1, done: false }

console.log(iterator.next());  // { value: 2, done: false }

console.log(iterator.next());[4]  // { value: 3, done: false }

console.log(iterator.next());  // { value: undefined, done: true[5] }
```

Using Iterators in `for...of` Loops

The `for...of` loop is a convenient way to iterate over iterables:

JavaScript

```javascript
const myArray = [1, 2, 3];



for (const value of myArray) {

  console.log(value); // 1, 2, 3

}
```

Creating Custom Iterables

You can create your own iterable objects by implementing the iterable protocol:

JavaScript

```javascript
const myIterable = {

  [Symbol.iterator]() {

    let index = 0;

    const data = [10, 20, 30];

    return {
```

```
    next() {

      if (index < data.length) {

        return { value: data[index++], done:
false };

      } else {

      return { done: true };

      }

    }

  };

  }

};


for (const value of myIterable) {

  console.log(value); // 10, 20, 30

}
```

Why Iterators and Iterables Matter in Asynchronous Programming

Lazy Evaluation: Iterators allow you to generate values on demand, which is useful for processing large datasets or streams of data without loading everything into memory at once.

Asynchronous Iteration: You can create iterators that produce values asynchronously, such as fetching data from an API in chunks.[6]

Control Flow: Iterators give you more control over the iteration process, allowing you to pause, resume, or skip values as needed.

By understanding iterators and iterables, you can write more efficient and flexible JavaScript code, especially when dealing with asynchronous operations and large datasets.

6.2 Generators: Pausing and Resuming Execution

Generators are special functions in JavaScript that can be paused and resumed during their execution. This unique capability makes them incredibly powerful for managing asynchronous control flow, especially when dealing with tasks that need to be performed in a specific order or when you want to process data in chunks.

Creating a Generator

You define a generator function using an asterisk (*) after the `function` keyword. Inside the generator, you use the `yield` keyword to pause execution and return a value.

JavaScript

```
function* myGenerator() {
```

```
    yield 1;

    yield 2;

    yield 3;

}
```

Using a Generator

Create a Generator Object: Call the generator function to create a generator object.

Call `next()`**:** Call the `next()` method on the generator object to start or resume execution. Each call to `next()` will execute code in the generator until it encounters a `yield` statement.

JavaScript

```
const gen = myGenerator();

console.log(gen.next());  // { value: 1, done: false }

console.log(gen.next());  // { value: 2, done: false }

console.log(gen.next());  // { value: 3, done: false }

console.log(gen.next());  // { value: undefined, done:[1] true }
```

Asynchronous Control Flow with Generators

Generators excel at managing asynchronous operations in a more controlled and sequential manner. Here's how:

Yielding Promises: You can `yield` a promise from within a generator. This pauses the generator until the promise resolves.

Iterating with `for await...of`**:** Use the `for await...of` loop to iterate over the generator. This loop automatically waits for each yielded promise to resolve before proceeding to the next one.

Example: Asynchronous Data Processing

JavaScript

```javascript
async function* processData(data) {

  for (const item of data) {

            const processedItem = await
someAsyncOperation(item); // Wait for async
operation

    yield processedItem;

  }

}
```

```
async function main() {

  const data = [1, 2, 3];

      for   await   (const   processedItem   of
processData(data)) {

    console.log(processedItem);

  }

}
```

Benefits of Generators for Asynchronous Control Flow

Improved Readability: Generators can make asynchronous code look more like synchronous code, improving readability and maintainability.

Sequential Execution: You can enforce a specific order of execution for asynchronous operations.

Pausing and Resuming: Generators allow you to pause and resume asynchronous tasks as needed, giving you more control over the flow.

Lazy Evaluation: Generators can generate values on demand, which is efficient for processing large datasets or streams of data.

Generators and Async/Await

While async/await is often the preferred choice for handling asynchronous code, generators offer a more powerful and flexible mechanism for controlling the flow of execution, especially when dealing with complex asynchronous patterns.

6.3 Real-World Applications of Generators

Generators, with their ability to pause and resume execution, offer unique solutions to various real-world problems. Here are some compelling examples of how generators are applied in practical scenarios:

1. Infinite Data Streams[1]

Generators can represent infinite sequences of data without consuming infinite memory.[2]

Example: Generating an infinite sequence of Fibonacci numbers:[3]

JavaScript

```javascript
function* fibonacci() {

  let a = 0, b = 1;

  while (true) {

    yield a;

    [a, b] = [b, a + b];

  }

}


const fib = fibonacci();
```

```
console.log(fib.next().value); // 0

console.log(fib.next().value); // 1

console.log(fib.next().value); // 1

console.log(fib.next().value);⁴ // 2

// ... and so on
```

2. Asynchronous Data Processing

Generators can simplify the processing of data that arrives in chunks or asynchronously, such as reading a large file or streaming data from an API.[5]

Example: Processing data from a stream:

JavaScript

```
async function* processStream(stream) {

  for await (const chunk of stream) {

    const processedChunk = await process(chunk);

    yield processedChunk;

  }

}
```

3. State Machines

Generators can effectively model state machines, which are systems that transition between different states based on events or inputs.[6]

Example: A simple traffic light state machine:

JavaScript

```javascript
function* trafficLight() {

  let state = 'red';

  while (true) {

    if (state === 'red') {

      yield 'red';

      state = 'green';

    } else if (state === 'green') {

      yield 'green';

      state = 'yellow';

    } else {

      yield 'yellow';

      state = 'red';

    }
```

}

}

4. Observables (RxJS)

Libraries like RxJS (Reactive Extensions for JavaScript) use generators to implement observables, which represent streams of asynchronous events or data.

5. Control Flow Management

Generators can be used to implement complex control flow patterns, such as coroutines or cooperative multitasking.[7]

6. Iterating Over Complex Data Structures

Generators can provide a convenient way to iterate over complex data structures, such as trees or graphs.[8]

7. Asynchronous Generators (Node.js)

In Node.js, asynchronous generators can be used to efficiently handle asynchronous operations that involve I/O, like reading from a database or making network requests.

Key Takeaways

Generators provide a powerful mechanism for managing asynchronous control flow and processing data in a more controlled and efficient manner.[9]

Their ability to pause and resume execution opens up possibilities for solving a wide range of problems in JavaScript.

Real-world applications of generators span from handling infinite data streams to implementing state machines and observables.

Chapter 7

Web Workers: Parallelism in JavaScript

7.1 Web Workers: JavaScript's Multithreading Solution

JavaScript, traditionally a single-threaded language, gained the ability to perform tasks concurrently with the introduction of Web Workers. Web Workers allow you to offload computationally intensive or long-running tasks to background threads, preventing them from blocking the main thread and keeping your web application responsive.

Why Offload Tasks?

Improved Performance: By moving heavy computations or operations to a separate thread, the main thread remains free to handle user interactions, UI updates, and other essential tasks. This prevents the browser from freezing or becoming sluggish.

Enhanced User Experience: Users experience a smoother and more responsive application, as the UI remains interactive even during intensive processing.

Better Resource Utilization: Web Workers can take advantage of multi-core processors, allowing you to parallelize tasks and utilize the full potential of the user's machine.

How Web Workers Work

Creating a Worker: You create a new worker using the `Worker` constructor, providing the path to a JavaScript file that contains the code to be executed in the worker thread.

JavaScript

```javascript
const worker = new Worker('myWorker.js');
```

Communicating with the Worker: You communicate with the worker using message passing:

Sending messages: Use the `postMessage()` method to send data to the worker.

Receiving messages: Listen for the `message` event on the worker to receive data back from the worker.

JavaScript

```javascript
// Main thread

worker.postMessage({ command: 'start', data: someData });



worker.onmessage = (event) => {

    console.log('Message from worker:', event.data);

};
```

```
// myWorker.js (Worker thread)

onmessage = (event) => {

  const data = event.data;

  // ... perform some task ...

  postMessage({ result: processedData });

};
```

Terminating a Worker: When you no longer need the worker, you can terminate it using the `terminate()` method.

JavaScript

```
worker.terminate();
```

Use Cases for Web Workers

Image and Video Processing: Manipulating images or videos can be computationally expensive. Web Workers can handle these operations in the background.

Data Analysis and Processing: Analyzing large datasets or performing complex calculations can be offloaded to workers.

Background Synchronization: Tasks like syncing data with a server can be performed in a worker without affecting the user interface.

Game AI: Complex game AI calculations can be handled in a separate thread to maintain smooth gameplay.

Limitations of Web Workers

Limited DOM Access: Web Workers cannot directly access the DOM (Document Object Model). They need to communicate with the main thread to update the UI.

No Access to Global Scope: Web Workers have their own global scope, separate from the main thread's global scope.

Data Transfer: Transferring large amounts of data between the main thread and workers can have performance implications.

Example: Calculating Fibonacci Numbers in a Worker

JavaScript

```
// main.js (Main thread)

const worker = new Worker('fibonacciWorker.js');



worker.postMessage({ number: 40 }); // Calculate
the 40th Fibonacci number



worker.onmessage = (event) => {

  console.log('Fibonacci result:', event.data);
```

```
};


// fibonacciWorker.js (Worker thread)

onmessage = (event) => {

  const number = event.data.number;

  function fibonacci(n) {

    if (n <= 1) return n;

    return fibonacci(n - 1) + fibonacci(n - 2);

  }

  const result = fibonacci(number);

  postMessage(result);

};
```

Web Workers are a valuable tool for improving the performance and responsiveness of your web applications. By understanding how to use them effectively, you can create a smoother and more efficient user experience.

7.2 Communicating with Web Workers

Web Workers operate in isolated threads, so they cannot directly access the main thread's variables or the DOM. Instead, communication relies on a message-passing model. This involves sending messages back and forth between the main thread and the worker.

Key Methods and Events

`postMessage()`: Used to send a message from either the main thread to the worker or vice versa. It accepts a single argument, which can be any data that is transferable (more on that below).

`onmessage`: An event handler that listens for incoming messages. The `event` object in the handler contains a `data` property, which holds the message received.

Example: Basic Communication

JavaScript

```
// main.js (Main thread)

const worker = new Worker('myWorker.js');




worker.postMessage('Hello    from    the    main
thread!');




worker.onmessage = (event) => {
```

```javascript
    console.log('Message       from       worker:',
event.data);

};



// myWorker.js (Worker thread)

onmessage = (event) => {

    console.log('Message    from    main    thread:',
event.data); // "Hello from the main thread!"

  postMessage('Hello back from the worker!');

};
```

Transferable Objects

For efficiency, especially when sending large amounts of data, you can use transferable objects. Transferable objects are transferred from one context (main thread or worker) to another, rather than being copied. This avoids the overhead of serialization and deserialization.

Examples of transferable objects:

```
ArrayBuffer
MessagePort
ImageBitmap
OffscreenCanvas
```

Example: Transferring an ArrayBuffer

JavaScript

```javascript
// main.js

const worker = new Worker('myWorker.js');

const buffer = new ArrayBuffer(1024);

worker.postMessage(buffer, [buffer]); // Transfer
ownership of the buffer

// myWorker.js

onmessage = (event) => {

  const receivedBuffer = event.data;

  // ... process the buffer ...

};
```

Important Considerations

Data Serialization: When sending non-transferable objects, they are serialized (converted to a string representation) before being sent and deserialized on the receiving end.

Asynchronous Nature: Message passing is asynchronous. You need to use callbacks or promises to handle responses from the worker.

Error Handling: Implement error handling in both the main thread and the worker to catch and handle any exceptions that might occur.

Structured Cloning Algorithm

When you send data using `postMessage()`, the data is cloned using the structured cloning algorithm. This algorithm can handle most data types, including:

Primitive types (numbers, strings, booleans)

Objects (including nested objects)

Arrays

Dates

Regular expressions

Blobs

FileLists

ImageData

However, it has some limitations:

Functions cannot be cloned.

DOM nodes cannot be cloned.

Error objects might not be cloned accurately.

By understanding the message-passing model and using the appropriate techniques, you can effectively communicate with Web Workers and leverage their power for concurrent processing in your web applications.

7.3 Use Cases for Improved Performance

Web Workers are excellent for boosting performance in web applications, especially when dealing with tasks that could otherwise block the main thread and lead to unresponsiveness.[1] Here's a breakdown of key use cases where Web Workers shine:

1. Intensive Computations

Complex Calculations: Offload tasks involving heavy mathematical computations, simulations, or data analysis to a Web Worker.[2] This prevents the browser from freezing while the calculations are performed.[3]

Examples: Generating fractals, performing scientific simulations, analyzing large datasets, cryptography.

Image and Video Manipulation: Image and video processing (resizing, filtering, encoding/decoding) can be resource-intensive.[4] Web Workers can handle these operations in the background, allowing for smooth UI interactions even when working with large media files.[5]

2. Background Data Processing

Fetching and Processing Large Datasets: When dealing with APIs that return large amounts of data, use a Web Worker to fetch and process the data in chunks.[6] This prevents the main thread from being blocked while waiting for the entire dataset to load.[7]

Pre-fetching Data: Load data in the background using a Web Worker to improve perceived performance. For example, pre-fetch data for the next page in a single-page application to enable faster navigation.

Data Synchronization: If your application needs to synchronize data with a server, perform the synchronization logic in a Web Worker to avoid disrupting the user experience.[8]

3. Games and Simulations

Game AI: Offload complex game AI calculations to a Web Worker.[9] This allows the main thread to focus on rendering the game and responding to user input, resulting in smoother gameplay.[10]

Physics Engines: Physics simulations in games can be computationally demanding.[11] Web Workers can handle the physics calculations separately, improving game performance.

4. Other Performance-Critical Tasks

Sorting and Searching: If your application involves sorting or searching large arrays or lists, delegate these operations to a Web Worker to maintain responsiveness.

String Manipulation: Complex string manipulation tasks (e.g., regular expression matching, text parsing) can benefit from being offloaded to a worker.

Web Scraping: Use Web Workers to perform web scraping operations in the background without affecting the user interface.[12]

Key Benefits for Performance

Concurrency: Web Workers enable true concurrency in JavaScript, allowing multiple tasks to run simultaneously.[13]

Responsiveness: By preventing long-running tasks from blocking the main thread, Web Workers ensure that the UI remains responsive and interactive.[14]

Resource Utilization: Web Workers can utilize multiple CPU cores, leading to more efficient use of system resources.[15]

By strategically using Web Workers for performance-critical tasks, you can significantly enhance the speed and responsiveness of your web applications, providing a better user experience.[16]

Chapter 8

Diving Deep into Event Emitters

8.1 Understanding the Observer Pattern

The Observer pattern is a powerful behavioral design pattern that allows objects to communicate and stay in sync without being tightly coupled. It defines a one-to-many relationship between objects:

Subject: The object being observed. It maintains a list of its dependents, called observers, and notifies them automatically of any state changes.

Observers: Objects that are interested in the state changes of the subject. They register themselves with the subject to receive updates.[1]

How it Works

Registration: Observers register their interest with the subject, typically by providing a callback function or implementing an interface.

Notification: When the subject's state changes, it notifies all registered observers by calling their callback functions or the appropriate methods defined in the interface.

Update: Observers receive the notification and can then take appropriate actions based on the updated state of the subject.

Benefits of the Observer Pattern

Loose Coupling: The subject and observers are loosely coupled. The subject doesn't need to know the specific implementation details of its observers. This promotes modularity and flexibility.

Dynamic Relationships: Observers can be added or removed at runtime without affecting the subject or other observers.

Scalability: The pattern can handle a large number of observers efficiently.

Event Handling: The Observer pattern is often used to implement event handling systems, where objects need to react to various events or state changes.

Example: News Publisher and Subscribers

Imagine a news publisher (subject) and subscribers (observers).

Subject (NewsPublisher):

Has a list of subscribers.

Provides methods for subscribers to subscribe and unsubscribe.

Notifies subscribers when new news is available.

Observer (NewsSubscriber):

Has a method to receive news updates (e.g., `update(news)`).

Subscribes to the NewsPublisher to receive updates.

JavaScript

```
class NewsPublisher {
```

```
constructor() {

  this.subscribers = [];

}



subscribe(subscriber) {

  this.subscribers.push(subscriber);

}



unsubscribe(subscriber)² {

                    this.subscribers      =
this.subscribers.filter(sub     =>     sub     !==
subscriber);³

  }



notifySubscribers(news) {

      this.subscribers.forEach(subscriber   =>
subscriber.update(news));

  }
```

```javascript
}


class NewsSubscriber {

  constructor(name) {

    this.name = name;

  }



  update(news) {

      console.log(`${this.name}  received  news:
${news}`);

  }

}



// Usage

const publisher = new NewsPublisher();

const subscriber1 = new NewsSubscriber('Alice');

const subscriber2 = new NewsSubscriber('Bob');
```

```
publisher.subscribe(subscriber1);

publisher.subscribe(subscriber2);


publisher.notifySubscribers('Breaking news!');

  // Output:

// Alice received news: Breaking news!

// Bob received news: Breaking news!
```

Real-World Applications

UI Frameworks: React, Angular, and Vue.js use the Observer pattern to update the UI in response to data changes.

Event Handling: Browser events (clicks, mouseovers, keyboard input) are handled using the Observer pattern.

Social Media: Notifications and updates in social media platforms are often implemented using the Observer pattern.

Stock Market: Stock tickers and price updates can be modeled using the Observer pattern.

The Observer pattern is a fundamental design pattern that promotes loose coupling and efficient communication between objects, making it a valuable tool in many software development scenarios.

8.2 Building Custom Event Emitters

While JavaScript provides built-in event handling mechanisms (like the `addEventListener` method for DOM events), there are times when you need more fine-grained control or want to create your own custom event systems. This is where building custom event emitters comes in handy.

Core Concepts

Event Emitter: An object that allows you to:

Register listeners (callbacks) for specific events.

Emit (trigger) events to notify listeners.

Listeners: Functions that are executed when a specific event is emitted.

Building a Custom Event Emitter

Here's a basic implementation of a custom event emitter in JavaScript:

JavaScript

```
class EventEmitter {

  constructor() {

    this.events = {}; // Store events and their
listeners
```

```
  }


  on(event, listener) {

    if (!this.events[event]) {

      this.events[event] = [];

    }

    this.events[event].push(listener);

  }



  emit(event, ...args) {

    if (this.events[event]) {

        this.events[event].forEach(listener  =>
listener(...args));[1]

    }

  }



  // Optional: Add methods for removing listeners
(off),
```

```
// listening only once (once), etc.

}
```

Explanation

`on(event, listener)`: Registers a listener function (`listener`) for a specific event (`event`).

`emit(event, ...args)`: Triggers an event (`event`) and passes any additional arguments (`...args`) to the registered listeners.

`events`: An object used to store events and their associated listeners.

Using the Custom Event Emitter

JavaScript

```javascript
const myEmitter = new EventEmitter();



// Register listeners

myEmitter.on('myEvent', (data) => {

    console.log('Event triggered with data:', data);

});
```

```
// Emit the event

myEmitter.emit('myEvent', 'Hello!'); // Output:
"Event triggered with data: Hello!"
```

Adding More Functionality

You can extend your custom event emitter with additional features:

`off(event, listener)`: Remove a specific listener for an event.

`once(event, listener)`: Register a listener that will be executed only once and then automatically removed.

Namespaces: Support namespaces in event names (e.g., `'user.login'`, `'user.logout'`) for better organization.

Error Handling: Add mechanisms to handle errors that might occur within listeners.

Benefits of Custom Event Emitters

Flexibility: You have complete control over how events are handled and propagated.

Modularity: Create decoupled components that communicate through events.

Reusability: Build a generic event emitter that can be used throughout your application.

Real-World Applications

Custom UI Components: Build interactive UI components with custom events for user interactions.

State Management: Create a central event emitter to manage application state changes and notify components.

Real-time Applications: Handle real-time events (e.g., chat messages, notifications) using a custom event emitter.

By understanding the Observer pattern and building your own custom event emitters, you can create more flexible, modular, and maintainable JavaScript applications.

8.3 Practical Applications in Node.js

Node.js, with its event-driven architecture, heavily relies on the Observer pattern and event emitters. Here are some practical applications of event emitters in Node.js:

1. Handling I/O Events

Many Node.js core modules, especially those dealing with input/output operations, use event emitters extensively.

File System Operations: The `fs` module emits events like `'open'`, `'close'`, `'error'`, and `'data'` when working with files.

JavaScript

```
const fs = require('fs');
```

```
const readStream =
fs.createReadStream('myFile.txt');
```

```
readStream.on('data', (chunk) => {
```

```javascript
  console.log('Received chunk:', chunk);

});
```

```javascript
readStream.on('end', () => {

  console.log('File read complete');

});
```

Network Operations: The `net` and `http` modules emit events for various network activities, such as `'connect'`, `'data'`, `'end'`, and `'error'`.

JavaScript

```javascript
const http = require('http');
```

```javascript
const server = http.createServer((req, res) => {

  // ... handle requests ...

});
```

```
server.on('request', (req, res) => {

  console.log('New request received');

});



server.listen(3000);
```

2. Building Custom Modules and APIs

Event emitters are essential for creating modular and well-structured Node.js applications.

Custom Modules: Design your modules to emit events to signal important occurrences or status changes, allowing other parts of your application to react accordingly.

API Design: Use event emitters to provide real-time updates or notifications to clients consuming your API.

3. Real-time Applications

Event emitters are a key component in building real-time applications with Node.js.

Chat Applications: Emit events for new messages, user presence updates, and other real-time interactions.

Collaboration Tools: Use event emitters to synchronize data and notify users of changes in collaborative environments.

Live Streaming: Emit events to signal the start, progress, and end of live streams.

4. Implementing the Observer Pattern

Event emitters provide a natural way to implement the Observer pattern in Node.js.

Subject: The object emitting the events acts as the subject.

Observers: Objects listening for events act as observers.

5. Monitoring and Logging

Event emitters can be used to create monitoring and logging systems.

Performance Monitoring: Emit events to track performance metrics and identify bottlenecks.

Error Logging: Emit events to log errors and exceptions for debugging and analysis.

Example: Custom Event Emitter for a Task Queue

JavaScript

```javascript
const EventEmitter = require('events');



class TaskQueue extends EventEmitter {

  constructor() {

    super();

    this.tasks = [];
```

```
    }


    addTask(task) {

      this.tasks.push(task);

      this.emit('taskAdded', task);

    }


    processTask() {

      if (this.tasks.length > 0) {

        const task = this.tasks.shift();

        this.emit('taskProcessed', task);

        // ... process the task ...

      }

    }

  }


  // Usage
```

```javascript
const queue = new TaskQueue();

queue.on('taskAdded', (task) => {

  console.log('New task added:', task);

});

queue.on('taskProcessed', (task) => {

  console.log('Task processed:', task);

});

queue.addTask('Task 1');

queue.addTask('Task 2');

queue.processTask();
```

By leveraging event emitters effectively, you can create more robust, modular, and real-time capable applications in Node.js.

Chapter 9

Reactive Programming with RxJS

9.1 Observables: Streams of Data Over Time

Imagine a stream of water flowing from a source. You can observe the stream, see the water flow by, and react to changes in the flow (like an increase or decrease in the water level). This is analogous to how observables work in reactive programming.

Definition: An observable is a stream of data that can be observed over time. It can emit zero or more values (of any type), and it can also signal completion or an error.

Key Concepts:

Emitting Values: Observables emit values over time. These values can be anything: numbers, strings, objects, events, etc.

Observers: Observers subscribe to observables to receive emitted values.

Operators: Operators are functions that transform or manipulate the stream of data emitted by an observable.

Subscriptions: A subscription represents the connection between an observer and an observable.

Creating an Observable

Here's a basic example using the RxJS library:

JavaScript

```
import { Observable } from 'rxjs';

const        myObservable        =        new
Observable(subscriber => {

  subscriber.next(1);

  subscriber.next(2);

  setTimeout(() => {

    subscriber.next(3);

        subscriber.complete();[1]  //  Signal
completion

  }, 1000);

});
```

Subscribing to an Observable

JavaScript

```
myObservable.subscribe({

    next: (value) => console.log('Received
value:', value),

    error: (err) => console.error('Error:',
err),
```

```
    complete: () => console.log('Observable
completed')

});



// Output:

// Received value: 1

// Received value: 2

// (after 1 second)

// Received value: 3

// Observable completed
```

Operators: Transforming Observables

Operators are the heart of reactive programming. They allow you to manipulate the stream of data emitted by an observable. RxJS provides a vast collection of operators for various purposes.

map: Transforms each emitted value.

JavaScript

```
myObservable.pipe(map(value => value * 2))
```

```
    .subscribe(value => console.lcg('Mapped
value:', value)); // 2, 4, 6
```

filter: Filters emitted values based on a condition.

JavaScript

```
myObservable.pipe(filter(value => value >
1))

    .subscribe(value => console.log('Filtered
value:', value)); // 2, 3
```

mergeMap: Combines multiple observables into one.

debounceTime: Delays emitted values to handle events like user input.

retry: Retries an observable if it encounters an error.

Why Observables and Operators Matter

Handling Asynchronous Events: Observables provide a unified way to handle asynchronous events, such as user input, network requests, and timers.

Managing Complex Data Flows: Operators make it easier to manage complex data flows and transformations.

Reactive Programming: Observables and operators are the foundation of reactive programming, a paradigm that focuses on reacting to data changes over time.

Real-World Applications

User Interfaces: React, Angular, and Vue.js use observables to manage UI updates in response to user interactions and data changes.

Real-time Applications: Handle real-time events (e.g., chat messages, stock prices) using observables.

Network Requests: Make and manage asynchronous network requests using observables.

By understanding observables and operators, you unlock the power of reactive programming and can build more dynamic and responsive applications.

9.2 Observables as Asynchronous Streams

In reactive programming with RxJS, observables are the primary way to handle asynchronous streams of data. They represent a sequence of values that are emitted over time, allowing you to react to these values as they arrive.

Key Concepts for Handling Asynchronous Streams

1 Subscribing to the Stream: To receive values from an asynchronous stream (observable), you need to subscribe to it. This establishes a connection between the source of the data and your observer (the code that will process the data).

2 Reacting to Emitted Values: When the observable emits a value, the `next()` method of your observer is called with the emitted value. You can then perform any necessary actions based on that value.

3 Handling Completion and Errors: Observables can signal completion (when there are no more values to emit) or an error. Your observer can include `complete()` and `error()` methods to handle these situations.

Example: Handling a Stream of Click Events

JavaScript

```javascript
import { fromEvent } from 'rxjs';



const button = document.getElementById('myButton');

const clicks$ = fromEvent(button, 'click');
// Create an observable of click events



const subscription = clicks$.subscribe({

    next: (event) => console.log('Button clicked:', event),

    error: (err) => console.error('Error:', err),
```

```
    complete: () => console.log('Click stream
completed')

    // (This might not happen for a button
click stream)

});
```

Operators for Stream Manipulation

RxJS provides a rich set of operators to manipulate and transform asynchronous streams. Here are some commonly used operators:

`map`: Transforms each emitted value.

`filter`: Filters values based on a condition.

`debounceTime`: Delays value emission, useful for handling user input.

`throttleTime`: Limits the rate of value emission.

`switchMap`: Switches to a new observable based on the emitted value.

`mergeMap`: Combines multiple observables into one.

`catchError`: Handles errors in the stream.

Example: Filtering and Mapping a Stream

JavaScript

```
import { of } from 'rxjs';

import { map, filter } from
'rxjs/operators';
```

```
const numbers$ = of(1, 2, 3, 4, 5);



numbers$.pipe(

    filter(value => value % 2 === 0), //
Filter even numbers

    map(value => value * 2)               //
Multiply even numbers by 2

)

.subscribe(value => console.log(value)); //
Output: 4, 8
```

Practical Applications

Real-time User Interfaces: Update the UI in response to a stream of user actions or data changes.

Data from WebSockets: Handle incoming messages from a WebSocket connection as a stream.

Progress Indicators: Display progress updates as a stream of events.

Infinite Scrolling: Load more data as the user scrolls, handling the incoming data as a stream.

Benefits of Using Observables

Composability: Operators allow you to compose complex stream transformations in a clear and readable way.

Error Handling: Observables provide mechanisms for handling errors that might occur in the stream.

Cancellation: Subscriptions can be canceled to stop receiving values from the stream.

Efficiency: Observables can handle backpressure (when the observer cannot process data as fast as it's emitted) to prevent overwhelming the system.

By understanding how to handle asynchronous streams of data using observables and operators, you can build more dynamic, responsive, and efficient applications.

9.3 Building Reactive Applications

Building reactive applications involves adopting a different mindset compared to traditional imperative programming. It's about creating systems that react to changes in data or events over time, resulting in more dynamic, responsive, and scalable applications. Here's a breakdown of the key concepts and steps:

1. Understanding Reactive Programming

Data as Streams: Think of data as continuous streams of values or events, rather than static variables.

Observables: Use observables (like those provided by RxJS) to represent these streams.

Operators: Employ operators to transform, combine, and manipulate the streams.

Observers: Define observers (callbacks) that react to the values emitted by the observables.

2. Choosing a Reactive Framework

While you can implement reactive programming principles without a framework, using one can significantly simplify the process. Popular choices include:

RxJS: A comprehensive library for reactive programming in JavaScript.

React: While not strictly a reactive framework, React's component-based architecture and unidirectional data flow align well with reactive principles.

Angular: Provides built-in support for RxJS and encourages reactive programming patterns.

Vue.js: Offers integration with RxJS and promotes reactivity through its reactivity system.

3. Designing Reactive Components

Component-Based Architecture: Break down your application into small, reusable components.

Unidirectional Data Flow: Ensure data flows in one direction, typically from parent components to child components.

State Management: Use a state management library (like Redux, MobX, or Vuex) to manage application state and trigger updates reactively.

4. Handling Asynchronous Operations

Observables for Asynchronicity: Use observables to represent asynchronous operations like network requests, user input events, and timers.

Operators for Control Flow: Employ operators like `mergeMap`, `switchMap`, and `catchError` to manage asynchronous control flow.

5. Testing Reactive Code

Marble Testing: Use marble testing techniques (provided by libraries like RxJS Marble Testing) to test your observables and operators.

Unit Tests: Write unit tests for your reactive components to ensure they behave as expected in response to data changes.

Example: Building a Simple Reactive Search

JavaScript

```javascript
import { fromEvent, debounceTime, map, switchMap } from 'rxjs';




const searchInput = document.getElementById('search');

const resultsContainer = document.getElementById('results');




const searchTerms$ = fromEvent(searchInput, 'input').pipe(

  debounceTime(300), // Debounce input events

  map(event => event.target.value), // Extract search term

  switchMap(searchTerm => fetch(`/api/search?q=${searchTerm}`)) // Make API request

);
```

```
searchTerms$.subscribe(response => {

  // Update resultsContainer with search results

  response.json().then(data => {

    // ... render search results in the UI ...

  });

});
```

Benefits of Reactive Applications

Increased Responsiveness: React to data changes and events in real-time, creating a more dynamic and interactive user experience.

Improved Code Maintainability: Reactive programming can lead to more modular, testable, and maintainable code.

Scalability and Performance: Observables and operators can help you manage complex data flows and asynchronous operations efficiently.

Simplified Asynchronous Programming: Observables provide a unified and powerful way to handle asynchronous operations.

Building reactive applications requires a shift in thinking, but the benefits in terms of responsiveness, maintainability, and scalability can be significant.

Chapter 10

Testing Asynchronous Code

10.1 Challenges in Testing Asynchronous Logic

Testing asynchronous logic in JavaScript presents unique challenges that differ from testing synchronous code. Here's a breakdown of the key hurdles and considerations:

1. Timing and Unpredictability

Non-Deterministic Execution: Asynchronous operations, like network requests or timers, don't execute in a predictable order. This makes it difficult to guarantee the state of your application at the time of your assertions.

Race Conditions: If your tests involve multiple asynchronous operations that interact, you might encounter race conditions where the order of completion affects the outcome. This can lead to flaky tests that pass or fail intermittently.

2. Testing Frameworks and Asynchronous Support

Test Framework Limitations: Not all testing frameworks have robust built-in support for asynchronous code. Older frameworks might require workarounds or manual handling of promises or callbacks.

Synchronization: You need mechanisms to ensure that your tests wait for asynchronous operations to complete before making assertions. This often involves using techniques like:

Callbacks: Passing callback functions to asynchronous operations to perform assertions after completion.

Promises: Using `.then()` or `async/await` to handle promise resolutions.

Framework-Specific Features: Leveraging features like `done()` callbacks (in Mocha) or `async/await` support in modern testing frameworks (Jest).

3. Mocking and Stubbing

External Dependencies: Asynchronous operations often involve external dependencies (e.g., APIs, databases). You need to mock or stub these dependencies to isolate your tests and avoid relying on external systems.

Timing Functions: Mocking timing functions like `setTimeout` or `setInterval` can be challenging. You might need specialized libraries or techniques to control their behavior in your tests.

4. Debugging and Troubleshooting

Error Handling: Asynchronous errors can be harder to track down. Ensure your tests have proper error handling to capture and report asynchronous exceptions.

Stack Traces: Asynchronous stack traces can be less informative than synchronous ones. Use debugging tools and techniques to understand the flow of execution in your asynchronous code.

5. Test Design and Structure

Isolation: Structure your tests to isolate asynchronous operations as much as possible to reduce complexity and improve reliability.

Focus on Behavior: Focus on testing the observable behavior of your asynchronous code rather than implementation details.

Example: Testing a Promise-Based Function

JavaScript

```javascript
async function fetchData() {

    // ... asynchronous operation that returns
    a promise ...

    }




    // Test using Jest

    test('fetchData should return the correct
    data', async () => {

      const data = await fetchData();

      expect(data).toEqual({ name: 'Alice', age:
    30 });

    });
```

Best Practices

Use a Modern Testing Framework: Choose a testing framework with strong support for asynchronous code (like Jest).

Mock External Dependencies: Isolate your tests by mocking external services.

Handle Promises and Callbacks: Use `async/await` or `.then()` to handle promises effectively in your tests.

Structure Tests Clearly: Write focused tests that isolate asynchronous logic.

Use Debugging Tools: Leverage debugging tools to understand asynchronous execution flow.

By understanding the challenges and best practices, you can write more effective and reliable tests for your asynchronous JavaScript code.

10.2 Using Jest for Asynchronous Testing

Jest is a popular JavaScript testing framework that provides excellent support for testing asynchronous code, making it easier to handle callbacks, promises, and async/await.[1] Here's how you can leverage Jest's features to write effective asynchronous tests:

1. Testing Callbacks

For older asynchronous patterns that use callbacks, Jest provides the `done()` callback.

Pass `done()` as an argument to your test function.

Call `done()` inside the callback of your asynchronous operation to signal that the test is complete.

If `done()` is not called within a reasonable timeout, the test will fail.

JavaScript

```javascript
test('fetchData with callback should return
correct data', (done) => {

  function fetchData(callback) {

    setTimeout(() => {

      const data = { name: 'Alice', age: 30
};

      callback(data);

    }, 1000);

  }


  fetchData((data) => {

    expect(data).toEqual({ name: 'Alice',
age: 30 });

    done();

  });

});
```

2. Testing Promises

Jest has built-in support for promises.[2] You can simply return a promise from your test function, and Jest will wait for it to resolve or reject.[3]

JavaScript

```javascript
function fetchData() {

  return new Promise((resolve) => {

    setTimeout(() => {

      const data = { name: 'Alice', age: 30
};

      resolve(data);

    }, 1000);

  });

}



test('fetchData with promise should return
correct data', () => {

  return fetchData().then(data => {

    expect(data).toEqual({ name: 'Alice',
age: 30 });
```

```
  });

});



// Or, using async/await:

test('fetchData   with   async/await   should
return correct data', async () => {

  const data = await fetchData();

  expect(data).toEqual({ name: 'Alice', age:
30 });

});
```

3. Testing Async/Await

Jest seamlessly handles `async/await`. Declare your test function as `async` and use `await` to wait for asynchronous operations.

JavaScript

```
test('fetchData   with   async/await   should
return correct data', async () => {

  const data = await fetchData();

  expect(data).toEqual({ name: 'Alice', age:
30 });
```

```
});
```

4. Resolves/Rejects Matchers

Jest provides `.resolves` and `.rejects` matchers to test the outcome of promises.

JavaScript

```
test('fetchData should resolve with correct
data', () => {

                                    return
expect(fetchData()).resolves.toEqual({ name:
'Alice', age: 30 });

});




test('fetchData should reject on error', ()
=> {

                                    return
expect(fetchDataWithError()).rejects.toThrow
('Network error');

});
```

5. Mocking Timers

Jest allows you to mock timers using `jest.useFakeTimers()` to control the execution of `setTimeout` and `setInterval` in your tests.

JavaScript

```
jest.useFakeTimers();


test('fetchData with mocked timer', () => {

    const callback = jest.fn();

    fetchData(callback);



    // Fast-forward time

    jest.advanceTimersByTime(1000);



        expect(callback).toHaveBeenCalledWith({
name: 'Alice', age: 30 });

    });
```

Benefits of Using Jest for Asynchronous Testing

Simplified Asynchronous Tests: Jest's built-in support for promises and async/await makes testing asynchronous code more intuitive.[4]

Improved Test Readability: Clearer test structure with less boilerplate code.[5]

Powerful Matchers: `.resolves` and `.rejects` provide concise ways to assert on promise outcomes.

Timer Mocking: Control time-dependent logic in your tests with Jest's timer mocks.[6]

By utilizing Jest's features, you can write more effective, readable, and maintainable tests for your asynchronous JavaScript code.[7]

10.3 Best Practices for Reliable Tests

Writing reliable tests for your JavaScript code, especially when dealing with asynchronous operations, is crucial to ensure the quality and stability of your applications.[1] Here are some best practices to keep in mind:

1. Focus on Testing Behavior

Black Box Testing: Treat the code you're testing as a "black box."[2] Focus on testing the external behavior and outputs of your functions or components, rather than their internal implementation details.[3] This makes your tests less brittle and more resistant to changes in the code.

Test Cases for Different Scenarios: Design test cases that cover a wide range of inputs, edge cases, and potential error conditions to ensure your code behaves correctly in various situations.

2. Structure and Organization

One Assertion per Test: Ideally, each test case should focus on a single assertion or expectation.[4] This makes it easier to understand what is being tested and to pinpoint the cause of failures.

Descriptive Test Names: Use clear and descriptive names for your test cases that convey the specific behavior being tested.[5] This improves the readability of your tests and makes it easier to understand their purpose.

Arrange, Act, Assert (AAA) Pattern: Follow the AAA pattern to structure your test cases:

Arrange: Set up the necessary preconditions and inputs for the test.

Act: Execute the code being tested.[6]

Assert: Verify the expected outcomes.[7]

3. Asynchronous Testing Techniques

`async/await`: Use `async/await` to write asynchronous tests that read like synchronous code, improving readability and maintainability.

Promises: Handle promises correctly using `.then()` or `async/await` to ensure your tests wait for asynchronous operations to complete before making assertions.

Callbacks: If working with callbacks, use the `done()` callback (in some testing frameworks) to signal test completion or leverage promises to manage the asynchronous flow.

4. Mocking and Stubbing

Isolate Dependencies: Mock or stub external dependencies (e.g., APIs, databases) to prevent your tests from relying on external systems and to control their behavior.[8]

Focus on Unit Testing: Use mocks and stubs to isolate the unit of code being tested, ensuring that your tests are focused and fast.[9]

5. Tools and Libraries

Modern Testing Framework: Choose a testing framework with robust support for asynchronous testing and features like mocking, stubbing, and code coverage (Jest is a good option).[10]

Assertion Library: Use an assertion library (like Chai) that provides a variety of assertions and helpful error messages.[11]

6. Code Coverage

Measure Coverage: Use code coverage tools to track how much of your code is being exercised by your tests.[12] Aim for high code coverage to increase confidence in your test suite.

7. Continuous Integration

Automate Testing: Integrate your tests into a continuous integration (CI) system to run them automatically on every code change, ensuring that your codebase remains stable and reliable.[13]

Example: Well-Structured Asynchronous Test

JavaScript

```
// Function to test
```

```javascript
async function fetchUserData(userId) {

    const response = await
fetch(`/api/users/${userId}`);

    return response.json();

}



// Test case using Jest

test('fetchUserData should fetch and return
user data', async () => {

    // Arrange

    const userId = 123;

    const mockUserData = { name: 'Alice',
email: 'alice@example.com' };

            global.fetch =
jest.fn().mockResolvedValue({

                            json:
jest.fn().mockResolvedValue(mockUserData)

    });



    // Act
```

```
        const    userData    =    await
fetchUserData(userId);



    // Assert


expect(fetch).toHaveBeenCalledWith(`/api/use
rs/${userId}`);

    expect(userData).toEqual(mockUserData);

});
```

By following these best practices, you can create a reliable test suite that helps you catch bugs early, ensures the quality of your code, and gives you confidence in making changes to your application.

www.ingramcontent.com/pod-product-compliance
Lightning Source LLC
LaVergne TN
LVHW052056060326
832903LV00061B/978